From Ordinary to *Extraordinary*

How I transformed my business in 12 months and how you can too!

Stefan Boyle

authorHOUSE®

AuthorHouse™ UK Ltd.
500 Avebury Boulevard
Central Milton Keynes, MK9 2BE
www.authorhouse.co.uk
Phone: 08001974150

First published by AuthorHouse   7/25/2011

ISBN: 978-1-4567-8167-5 (sc)
ISBN: 978-1-4567-8166-8 (e)

First published in Great Britain in 2011 by
PrintRepublic Ltd
Unit 4, Chiltern House,
Waterside,
Chesham
Bucks HP5 1PS
Tel 0845 862 5550
E: hello@printrepublic.co.uk

Marketing Guide for Small Business Owners

Simple Steps Guaranteed to Transform
You're Business from Just Ticking Over to
a Lead Generating
Money Making Machine!

INTRODUCTION

I will start with an unusual approach by asking you to only read this book if you are <u>serious</u> about your business and you are prepared to take definitive action!

If you own a Small to Medium Sized Business, and you are ready to take action, I can help, if you plan to make the following happen...

1. You want to grow your business
2. You want to change yourself and/or your business and take simple steps towards making a massive difference to the growth and profitability of your company
3. You want to learn any new ideas
4. You are ready to embrace change
5. You are aware ways that you have "always done it" may not be right so you want to explore new ideas

OK, I accept this is this is a slightly unusual way to start a marketing book, but if you do not want to make a difference to your business then please don't waste your time or money in buying and reading this book.

I am sure we have all met people (or recognise a trait in ourselves), where we say we want to take action but the reality is we never really do it. This book is all about implementing some simple techniques that will work as they are proven. If you are the type of person who is open to trying something different, then I hope you enjoy this book.

We have faced an incredibly tough economic climate in recent years which has affected many businesses of all sizes and we are still not out of the woods yet. So, we have to stand out from the crowd, think and act differently to how we have done before. If you are prepared to take this approach there is huge opportunity to thrive and grow your business and as our economy recovers and grows you will be in a position to maximise the potential of your business.

I'm a firm believer that you are totally accountable for your life. Take a grip of it and make a difference which can start just one step at a time, as long as those steps are positive and going in the right direction.

So I guess if you've read this far, the above factors do not apply to you. Well, if that's the case, welcome to the club of business owners who are trying to take positive action by learning and implementing new ideas to their business.

Maybe you are looking to start a business and want to go about it the right way. If that is true, well hats off to you and if you start as you mean to go on, I wish you well.

I will show you some simple techniques and actions any business owner can use to help grow their business quickly and how to continually drive new enquiries to their business.

I found something really exciting when I first learned these skills and tried and tested all of them and more myself. The techniques I show you in this book are relevant to any business and transferrable from industry to industry. Isn't that fantastic? I am not saying every single skill and technique is totally relevant to every business, but overwhelmingly the principles are relevant in some form or another and many are being applied to successful business often without real awareness of why and how they are working. So if we can analyse this and focus on the points that really can be successful, then it can have a massive impact. Well, I'm sure you will be the judge of that by the time you've read this book!

Ultimately, what sets successful business owners apart from others is their ability to confront difficulty and take action and get things done. If you can be brave enough to not make excuses, not wait for the exact right moment to start a business or to change your own business, there is no such thing as a perfect time and if you make it happen, then you deserve to enjoy success as many before and after you will not have the courage to do it!

I set out to transform my business from just another ordinary business into something extraordinary. Why settle for mediocrity when you can aim for the stars?!

It seems to me that so many business owners come in two categories. The first is those who either don't know what to do, have limited ambition or just simply can't be bothered to put the effort in. There are always some people, sadly quite a large majority who seem content with struggling by and always having an excuse or a reason as to why things aren't quite happening for them.

It's often the economy, their competitors, suppliers and raw materials are too expensive, it's quiet because it's too hot, it's too cold, it's holiday season... you know what I'm getting at and the type of excuses that are given.

The second type are those who strive for success, are totally driven and are hungry for knowledge and never want to stop learning and investing in themselves.

To me, if you are taking the time to read this book, you are the latter. I personally would like to say I too am in that category.

My wife thinks I'm some kind of business book worm!

I am always buying new business books, reading websites and blogs, watching videos.

I try and absorb as much as possible and learn everything I can from those who have been there and done it.

It's great to get a whole range of ideas and really think about what you agree with, what is relevant to you and your market and to actually implement them.

Owning a business is a fantastic journey of highs and lows and you can never sit on your laurels and think you've made it.

The world changes, technology changes and as business owners we have to make sure we strive to stay one step ahead. If you think about all the successful businesses you have known within your network, how many have you seen come and go?

I have seen dozens!

Then think about technologies that come along, people make fortunes and then something new overtakes it and they are left behind.

The music industry is a classic case and think how that market place has dramatically been affected. Not only the stores that sold CD's but I knew a number of highly successful CD production companies who are either gone or significantly smaller than they were only a few years ago.

So it is vital you learn, take nothing for granted, develop and evolve to ensure you and your business ride the crest of new and developing markets and not dying ones!

Industries and customer needs and wants change, businesses must continually evolve to carry on competing and innovating as nothing stays the same forever.The beauty of the skills I teach you in this book is how they can be applied to almost any business, in almost any sector.

I hope this book sets you the same journey and helps you put in place some easily implementable strategies that will ultimately result in your business being extraordinary too!

Good luck
Stefan

Contents

What other readers have said....

Read and learn how easily 'ordinary' becomes 'extraordinary'!

This book is for the ordinary business owner, with an ordinary business, working too many ordinary hours for a disappointingly ordinary return. This is for the business owner who feels that there must be EXTRAORDINARY path out there somewhere but needs a hand finding it. Read this book and give its strategies a go and learn how easily ordinary becomes extraordinary!
Wendy Shand, Founder and Director, www.totstotravel. co.uk

When I first met Stefan, he was a frustrated and stressed Business Owner who was looking to improve himself and his business. I have genuinely seen him transform himself and his business by learning new marketing skills that every business owner should know. Stefan has changed his total approach and the results are significant. Read Stefan's book and take his inspiration to transform your business
Jonathan Jay, Managing Director www.nabo.biz

"Let's just do it" is packed full of invaluable common sense marketing tips for small businesses. Stefan's energy and enthusiasm jumps out of the pages and his business is a credible partnership to any business wanting to grow."

"Print Republic is certainly not just another printer, they have a deep knowledge and understanding as to why and how their products are being used. Most importantly they totally understand ROI and know that to build lasting relationships with their customers the print material and on line marketing materials must offer an ROI so they

really want your marketing to work for you, they will do everything they can to make sure you get the results you want and more."
Sam Anderson, Managing Director, Post & Packaging Services Ltd

A "No BS", action orientated way to grow your business blowing a way the mystic of on line marketing and the Marketing Directors excuse of "you can't measure the benefit" from a guy who understands the up and downs of growing SME businesses.
Chris Cole, Director, www.MakeitCheaper.com

Most small and medium sized businesses know they need marketing but they just don't know where to start. Most have limited budgets and can't see how they could possibly afford to spend on marketing. As a consequence, they do nothing. Stefan's book gives you the step by step guide that you need to get started and shows you how you don't need to spend huge sums of money to get started. Most importantly he tells you how to measure the effectiveness of your marketing and get a return on your investment.

This book is a must read for any business owner who wants to grow their business and is willing to take action.
Rob Andrews, Managing Director - Lauder Beaumont Associates

This book is packed with easy to follow practical advice that is relevant in today's marketplace.

The style of writing makes it a pleasure to read and clearly indicates that you have built your business by practising what you preach.

Anybody who has the ambition to accelerate the growth of their business should read this book and get immediately into action.

The powerful techniques described in such detail cost very little to implement but produce tangible and very profitable results!
Dave Reynolds, www.DaveReynolds.com

This book is essential reading for all business owners who want to make a difference to themselves and their business. Stefan's book gives some great tips and ideas that I have now used and I recommend it for anyone who wants to grow their business and become true marketers. Easy to read, easy to understand and easy to implement but these ideas can truly make a significant difference to any small business!
Simon Duce, Managing Director, www.arpm.co.uk

Stefan has written the modern-day marketing equivalent of the Cheats guides that school boys use for English Literature exams: What you absolutely must know if you run an SME, the strategies, tools and mindset that separate you from your competitors. How does he know? Because he's actually tried and tested these insights in his business and with his customers. Not only has he shared plenty of valuable knowledge but also some of the key tools that you need to make it happen. A cracking little book !
Andy Gooday, Managing Director www.MarcatusHq.com

CHAPTER ONE:
So who on earth are you?!

That's a question I ask myself before reading a new book by an author I don't know. For me, it is always good to understand a bit more than the jargon that publishers and PR people put together so you can see if you can relate to the person who's sharing their knowledge and experience with you.

So who am I?

I am just a normal, average bloke who is continually learning about himself and trying to always learn a better way to improve myself and my business.

When I first met a well-known marketer called Peter Thompson he told a simple story in comparing learning and coaching for the world's elite sports men and women to those of us in business and everyday life.

Peter said, when Tiger Woods has his worst ever round of golf, he goes to the practice ground with his coach and analyses what went wrong. When Tiger has his best ever round, he goes to the practice ground with his coach and analyses what went right.

He practises and learns every day.

Now maybe Tiger could have done with some more coaching in his personal life but that is beside the point. There is no disputing the point that for many years he has totally dominated his chosen sport and he has been probably the world's number one sporting figure. Amazing achievements but he is still learning.

So why do so many people who own businesses think they know enough to remain solitary in their own world and try and just carry on regardless?

If you think about it, what we all need to do is keep on learning from our mistakes and from others who have already made mistakes and are happy to help others to find a better way.

Now where have I come from?

I have always been interested in business. If I could turn back the clock, I would have paid far more attention at school and got better grades than I did, but I always had the attitude that what I was learning was not going to really help me in my career.

I always just knew that I was more interested in work and a career than academia alone. I think this was naïve in hindsight but that is just how I was.

Still today, I see so many young people going to University to do mediocre degrees and leave expecting to get a great job but are sadly disappointed when they find themselves taking any work they can and not walking straight into a dream job!

I would still encourage any young person who is similar to how I was and not massively academic, to go and find the right career path and get cracking, rather than build up huge student debt that becomes a burden to them for years and also find themselves several paces behind others who are already making progress in business.

Although I went to college to study printing for two years, I learnt more in my first six months in a proper job than in the whole of my college course!

I was lucky enough to be able to work part time when I was at college in my Dad's business. I worked on the factory floor and that was a real help to giving me an understanding of the work environment and I think that was a big help when I started looking for a job.

In the late eighties when I started work, jobs were abundant in printing and I went to eight job interviews and was offered every job! Although I would obviously put that down to my sheer and utter brilliance, the reality is there was a real demand for people in a thriving industry.

Sadly, this is a huge reversal of the current state of play in the printing where technology has ravaged the industry.

So after college I was lucky enough to get a good job and after a year there, I had saved up enough money to go travelling... London to Kathmandu on a London Double Decker bus!

That experience was life changing and I would still recommend young people travelling as it simply broadens your horizons to what an amazing place the world is and there is so much to see.

I returned and walked into another job, where I repeated the cycle of a year's work and then upped and left to go to the Far East and Australia for another adventure.

I like to look at these trips as my visit to the University of Life and they were fabulous carefree days, meeting some great people and seeing some incredible sights.

But when I returned in 1991, the economy was not quite as vibrant and the quickest way into a job was to work for my Dad until I went out and got a proper job! I was there 17 years so I am still looking!

Working for my Dad who was self-taught in business was a great experience. Someone, who by his own admission, had a limited education but against some incredible odds, managed to start his own printing business and had more success in a small business than almost anyone I know. I am sure you have heard people talk about wanting to start a business or do something significant in their life but always find excuses. Well, if you are serious, you find a way.

When my Dad started his business literally in his garden shed at nights as well as holding down a day job, I had just been born. I was not a well baby from the start, having a serious emergency operation at just 2 weeks old and spent time in Great Ormond Street Hospital with pneumonia amongst other things.... Obviously I recovered as you can see! My Mum was also extremely unwell at this time and had a kidney removed and there was obviously huge strain on my family as a whole.

But my Dad persevered and worked all the hours he could, despite that, after seven years, his accountant told him to pack up as he was not going to succeed. Thankfully he ignored this advice and would not give up and went on to achieve some great success.

We have all heard the phrase "where there's a will there's a way". If you want an excuse, you can find one but with determination, you can overcome incredible odds.

My Dad worked on some strong principles that he adhered to without wavering and this ensured his business thrived, and as a result he built a strong financial bedrock into his business that never wavered. He was, and still is a highly successful businessman who ensured he thrived in a time where the industry he was in was in its golden years. Even in the golden years for the print industry, there were, of course varying degrees of success.

Many people failed and many people did well, but he focussed not on necessarily growing his business at all costs, but on profitability and building an extremely strong asset base that continues to grow in value to this day where many other businesses faded away.

I learnt an awful lot from my Dad and still try to apply some of his principles into my business, but I wanted to put my own imprint on the world and in business. Having worked for him for 17 years, to be honest, I felt I needed to change and more than anything I wanted to be in control of my own destiny.

We went through a transitional period where I bought the business from my Dad and this proved to be a difficult time for all of us. Sadly this period in my family's life was a difficult one but at the same time it was a time where I learnt an awful lot about myself and also to face up to the fact that nothing is forever and you have to make changes both to your life and your business.

Whilst not wanting to go into too much personal detail here, I think both I and my Dad made mistakes that we would both probably not make again. I don't know anyone who has not had some form of family fallout or arguments over the years, but when your life is engrained and revolves around a business, any turmoil affects everyone involved.

In my experience, both in my own family business and the knowledge I have of other family businesses, when things are good, there is nothing better. When things go wrong, it can have a major impact on your life.

I think it is only fair to say that succession planning in business, particularly in family run situations, is a vital activity that must be clear and transparent to the relevant parties. I guess that was one of the fundamental problems there was for me in my family business.

The simplest way I can explain it, if you have children, it is often a parental view that even when they are adults, they are still your kids!

This is fine and endearing and completely understandable in general terms, but in a work environment it isn't really ideal. I have two lovely girls who are still young but I guess I will always see them as my babies! Hence, I am not making plans for them to go into my business!

I can't complain about the situation I found myself in at our family business as I was given an opportunity by my parents and I would like to think I made the most of it and everyone benefitted in one way or another. If it wasn't for the time I had working for my Dad, I would have not learned what I have and we would all change certain things about our past.... But none of us can so we have to move forward.

I think it is hard for a parent to let go of your kids and as many of you with their own businesses, this may be a similar issue. When you start a business, it needs nurturing, attention and is also extremely hard work. Many people see a business like it's their "baby". I do meet other people who are far more practical and have a 5 year plan for a business and have a clear exit strategy. Very clear aims and goals from the start.

I am far more like this now but who is to say what is right and wrong. Is Rupert Murdoch wrong to have worked to old age in his business and not got out and sold up? It seems to have worked pretty well for him whether you like him or not!

My Dad was one of those people who really nurtured his business and I think it was really difficult to let it go. The problem was that I wanted complete control.

I didn't want to have to ask my Dad for a pay rise or on major decisions in the business. Maybe I inherited a "control freak gene" too because my Dad had no-one to answer to and I guess I am much the same.

This issue of not wanting to let go on my Dad's part and me wanting to be independent and achieve success off my own back and not fall into the trap that many people who get involved with family businesses often do.

My view was (and still is), my Dad's success was my Dad's success. I never wanted to hang off those shirt tails. I never cared if I inherited a penny, as long as my parents went out and spent every penny having the life of riley and enjoying the freedom, choice, independence and fun that hard work and success brings you.

This issue eventually came to a head and caused a pretty traumatic time that still has had a knock on effect even now, but life has moved on and I had to do it. Of course hindsight is a great thing and we would all change things with that benefit but regret is not something that is a healthy thing to live with as we would all change certain actions we have made if we could turn back the clock.

So the short story is I eventually bought the business off my Dad.

But this was still not the only difficulty I faced.

For the industry in which I started the foundations of my career in, printing, there have been massive changes. From the obvious impact of technology and the explosion in online communications the knock on effect is that many businesses have focussed their marketing budgets on web development and online marketing, which in turn has had a huge negative effect on their printing budgets and requirements.

Coupled with the fact that many of our clients were in the financial services sector and the credit crunch simply decimated a large proportion of our client base almost overnight!

I was in a situation that I had not experienced before, thinking I had a pretty good business head but not knowing what to do for the best. If you have been in that place you will understand how I was feeling.

This is an extremely stressful place to be. Of course people have worse scenarios so let's get this in some perspective.

But my guess is if you are taking the time to read this book you are like me in the sense that business is your passion and success is the driving force in your life. The desire to build a successful business and have the lifestyle and freedom that goes hand in hand with that is really the dream and the fire in our bellies!

For me, success is not just about building wealth, it is primarily about freedom and choice. If you build a fantastic business that you are proud of, inevitably the financial reward follows.

This reward may not be just about financial gain if you have other significant priorities but the bottom line is, the success you aim to achieve will give you the opportunity to choose what you want to do with your life.

So I knew that to achieve the success I wanted I had to make some changes.

I knew I had to get back to basics and learn some new skills. Like everyone who reads this book who currently owns a business of their own, we all have our expertise in the sector and we know the products and services we provide are top notch.

The problem that I see time after time in small and medium sized businesses is that they do not know how to market themselves properly.

I too was in that position. So I decided to do something about it!

I had spent thousands on marketing, websites, advertising, sales reps that were full of excuses about how we were too expensive, the market was quiet blah blah blah!

I was fed up and demotivated. Working all the hours, seeing less of my young family and getting more and more stressed!

In fact I started to become someone who I didn't actually like very much. Stress can have a massive impact in your life both in your behaviour and also potentially on your health. The stress of business being so tough combined with the burning desire for success and the rewards it brings that all of us who are ambitious put upon ourselves.

Can you relate to this?

If so, I am pleased you are reading this and trying to do something about it.

I knew I had to change. I needed to learn new skills and implement them in my business and quickly!

So I decided that massively improving my marketing skills was going to be the key area for both myself and my business. If I was going to be able to change how I work and how I run my business, I needed to get better at marketing and make sure I communicated the right messages, at the right time to the right people.

So I started investigating the opportunities to learn about marketing.

I got off my backside and went to a seminar where I met a man called Jonathan Jay who runs an excellent business growth organisation. I signed up for one of Jonathan's marketing programmes and absorbed as much as I could.

As well as all the skills Jonathan teaches, he also encourages you to read as many marketing books as possible and I now continually buy new marketing books and learn as much as I can on a regular basis. I urge you to do the same.

I think it is fair to say, that Jonathan had a massive influence on me in what he teaches and he helped give me direction and the confidence to carry on the path I had started on myself, as I was still not sure exactly which road I needed to take when there were a number of routes in front of me.

I have been to countless other seminars and training sessions by the best marketers I could find and I absorbed (and still do) every skill and insider technique I can get my hands on.

Shares in Amazon must have increased as I seem to continually buy marketing and business books and keep on learning by reading books by the world's leading authorities on marketing!

I mix with many like-minded business people and thrive on the advice, input and assistance I get from my trusted friends and colleagues. Building a strong and reliable peer group who get to know you well, understand your business and are honest enough to tell you when you are walking along the wrong path but also celebrate the successes along the way is just as rewarding as every penny you earn.

If you have these strong relationships with other business owners and help them with their business too, as you see them progress, succeed and thrive it is equally as rewarding.

I urge you to build your own mini mastermind groups that you meet up with regularly and you gain each other's trust – if you have some structure and aim to really make progress, it's hugely worthwhile and rewarding for all concerned.

Knowledge is fantastic and it arms you with skills and ideas although there is one more thing that is absolutely vitally important above everything else once you start working out how you can implement these skills in your business.

You absolutely must, without exception...

Take Massive Action!

If you learn all these new skills but do nothing with them, you have to an extent wasted your time. In the same vein, I see many business people who come up with a marketing idea and then try to over analyse and fine tune it again and again and again.... before they actually (if ever) roll it out.

Inevitably often it never happens as the best way to learn and make progress is by making decisions and implementing them quickly and then developing them as you gain knowledge from the results.

When you learn, then you fine tune and then you do it again but a little bit better than the previous time. But importantly, you are making progress.

In this book, I aim to give you a good foundation knowledge of some key activities and strategies that if you want to own a growing business, you <u>must</u> implement.

A business that is not growing and developing is in effect going backwards!

It is vital to remain positive even when you are up against it and the odds are against you. Running a business can be a lonely place sometimes and you have to make tough decisions. I have experienced this first hand when I decided to close part of my business and I had to lose some good people. It's never easy but if you know your goals and work towards that vision relentlessly, decisions become easier to make.

If I asked you take just one thing from this book, it's to make sure you make decisions and implement them.

Procrastination is a dangerous thing and believe me, I know, it has been one of my worse traits although I would probably need another book to list them all out!

But I have learnt to change how I work, I have learnt new skills and I apply them quickly into my business, ranging from what we do on a day to day basis, how we market and communicate our key messages and how I now operate differently in my company, working on the business instead of engrossed in it.

In my business we are generating hundreds of leads every month for new business opportunities. By implementing all of the techniques I will explain to you in this book, my business has transformed which as a knock on effect has totally changed how I feel about it.

Of course I still work hard as I am striving to achieve even greater goals, but my strategy is now to orchestrate my business and that old cliché to "work on it rather than in it".

I urge you to take on board and implement as many of the ideas and actions I recommend in this book and I am sure you will be delighted with the difference it makes to both you and your business.

Have you heard the saying "if it's to be, it's down to me"?

It's true!

Learn, take action and make it happen!

CHAPTER TWO:

You are wasting every penny you spend on advertising!

Sorry to say that but if you are not measuring exactly what return you get for your advertising, you are quite possibly wasting every penny!

Trust me you are not alone!

The vast majority of Small to Medium Sized Enterprises (SME's) are in the same boat. How many times have you placed an advert or sent out a direct mail piece or brochure and had a terrible response?

My hand is up for a start because I have learnt the hard way. I have quite simply wasted thousands of pounds on advertising by not measuring the response, not really understanding what I want to achieve and by focussing on promoting my own company and not thinking what my customers and prospects want and need.

Well I'll be amazed if you can say hand on heart that advertising has always worked fantastically well because quite frankly, most business people I speak to are more often than not disappointed by the return on investment of their marketing spend.

So why is that?

There is a common symptom that too many companies are marketing their business using Icon or Brand Advertising and many people re-assure themselves when their marketing fail to generate a response that "it's ok, at least I generated some brand awareness"

Now, I know the truth hurts, but if you come into this category, you're kidding yourself and more importantly you're wasting your money!

Brand awareness is not an activity that will make money for SME's, it is for businesses like Nike, DHL, Coca Cola, Marks & Spencer, Google etc. I'm sure you get the picture. These companies have monumental marketing budgets and they are trying to in effect brainwash people into thinking of their product over every one of their competitors.

There is not necessarily a direct correlation between this form of advertising and performance but it does make your company look good if you have the huge budgets to continually deliver your messages and company image to your prospective clientele.

For SME's it is very difficult to justify spending large sums on Branding and Advertising when it's possible to do it for affordable expenditure. It's important to have consistency across every touchpoint of your business – from your letterhead, signage, website, brochure etc. and to create an image that reflects the tone of business and industry you are in.

For example, if you run a kids party playhouse business –if you have got kids I'm sure you know the type of thing with ball pits and climbing frames and slides where they should give free headache tablets for parents who have to endure them! Well this business will probably try and create a kind of wacky and fun logo, image and name. Possibly cartoon like and really appeal to kids.

Now imagine if an accountancy practice attempted the same type of look! Would they be taken seriously? Of course not and I know this is a slightly ridiculous comparison but it demonstrates the concept.

You may have to think about the ideal prospect you are targeting and think about what tone and approach that would appeal to them. Remember you can't please all the people all the time but who you need to appeal to is the people who have a need and a requirement for your product and service.

You need to think about the key items you need to produce to give you a consistent image and write them down. This will probably start with your logo and the visual identity of the business which can lead on to branding, values, maybe a strapline (this is a huge subject in itself), business stationery, website and some marketing literature.

There are ways to get optimum value when you buy bundled offers from graphic design and printing companies and aside from the cost, the key is consistency so you don't confuse your prospects. There are many specialist companies in each individual area of online design, offline design and production but it's vital the left hand knows what the right hand is doing so there is consistency across the board.

It can often be sensible to do some research and try and find a company that can handle a project like this from start to finish so there is complete accountability with them for consistency.

So let's assume you have chosen a company to design your logo, your identity and the overall feel of your brand. You have some nice stationery and you are proud of your business so you want to get out there and market the hell out of it to get some great customers.

How do you **NOT** waste your advertising budget?

Well now is where you need to think differently. You need to set yourself apart from the crowd. You need to ask yourself a seemingly obvious question....

Who exactly is your customer?

Now the answer cannot be "well anyone" or "any business as all businesses require our widgets". You must drill down much further than this. Even if you can in theory provide almost anyone with your product or service there is one vital thing to consider before you do any advertising at all

What is your NICHE?

I cannot re-iterate how vital it is to target a definitive sector. Become the specialist supplier to a sector by telling them you are the Expert in their marketplace.

If you are an accountant, become the Experts in Tax Management for Farmers, or if you are a Business Consultant, specialise in working for widget manufacturers.

Why is it vital to Niche?

If you really know who you are targeting, it is much easier to get to them. If you are targeting farmers, you can find out what trade associations they are members of, what websites they visit, what magazines they read, what exhibitions they attend.

Then, you need to create an irresistible offer that makes it a no brainer for them to try your company.

Niche marketing really helps you drill down to thinking about your target prospect and building everything you do around that market place.

The real beauty of finding a profitable niche that you can really service well, is it is far easier to dominate that market, rather than just going for everyone!

Aim to be the biggest fish in that small pond!

If you can make your products or service really appeal to everyone in a small sector, you will become the company of choice to those people.

You can also raise your own profile to becoming the expert in your field and before you know it, you will be able to dominate that market.

Now many business owners think that as their products or services are suitable to anyone, how on earth can they niche?

Well, lots of people are in that same position. For example, restaurants could in theory serve anyone and everyone. But then again you get different types such as Italian, Indian, Chinese etc.

Then again, there are even smaller niches like Vegetarian and Vegan, organic only, Child friendly, Indonesian, Nepalese... the list goes on but I am sure you get the point.

Each of these restaurants will appeal to different people at different times.

The same appeals to mechanics or car retailers. You see some mechanics that are just your run of the mill servicing centre. Others specialise in Aston Martins, or vintage cars and you know instantly where you would go if you had that sort of car. You wouldn't go to them with a run of the mill family saloon car, but it you had a beautiful vintage car it would be highly likely that you would want a specialist company to look after it.

That can be niched even further if the mechanic specialised in vintage Alfa Romeos, Rolls Royce or Jaguars.

So in your business how can you really focus your marketing down to a niche?

One of the first things to think about in your niche is if it will be profitable!

There is absolutely no point in thinking about targeting a niche who don't have any money to spend!

Don't forget that there are niches within niches! You could start with professional services. So within that there are solicitors. You could then drill down to solicitors who have a specialist area such as maybe divorce, conveyancing, or property. Then you could think of an area, or size of firm and number of partners.

It's amazing how often you can start talking to a business owner who says they can provide their products and services to anyone and when you talk about their current clients they already have a great niche but they hadn't actually thought about it before!

Often a niche to a current business is there already as it is usually in the area where they have had most success, sometimes by luck alone, but who cares, make the most of it.

What is fantastic when you know where your niche is you can really start thinking how you can talk to those people.

You can pretty easily workout where your target prospects go both on and offline. For example, what magazines do they read? What exhibitions do they attend? What websites to they visit most?

What is the biggest problem those prospects face?

If you can establish this, your advertising can explain how you can solve this and you will also know where to advertise!

It's pretty simple but it is vital to get this right!

So your adverts and sales letters need to focus on some key factors to draw in your prospects. Your sales letters need to be key and you can use elements of them to create adverts.

There is a fundamental structure that will help you write great sales letters.

This is the basis you can work from:-

- Strong Captivating **Headline** that captures attention instantly and makes people read on.
- Create a **story** that sets the scene and talks about the prospects problem. Occasionally the prospect may not even know it's a problem until you highlight it!
- Write some **content** that describes what you or your product does
- Detail the key **benefits** and create desire
- Show **Proof** – examples of ways in which this has worked for other people and probably testimonials from happy customers
- Make them a great *Irresistible Offer* that will tempt them to buy
- **Guarantees** that make it an easy decision for them
- Call to **Action**, often quite simply being direct and telling people clearly what they must do. Often it works to create some scarcity with either a time limit on the offer or a limited number of products / customers

What is an irresistible offer?

You have to make it so easy and risk free for customers to start a trading relationship with you so once they are over that initial hurdle, it is far easier to get them coming back for more.

I am sure you have seen all the deals around where you can pay nothing for 14 days, or try before you buy and if you don't like the products you can return them without any obligation. Well the reason there are so many of this type of irresistible offers is because quite simply they work!

The number of people who bother to return products is negligible, especially if your product or service is of a high quality.

Take a look at your client list if you are an established business and look for trends where you have had best success. You may well discover that you are winning business in a certain sector, but actually you hardly make any money. If this is the case, then get out of this sector.

Look for areas in your business where you make the most money with both the products and services you sell as well as the customers you provide who are willing to pay a fair price for the value you provide. Get rid of the products and services you provide and for the customers with whom you make no profit, either charge a higher price or let them go!

Do it! It's liberating!

CHAPTER THREE:

How to get your website visitors attention immediately

I have met so many business owners who have a website because they just think they have got too as other people do.

In many cases it is a typical brochure site, that is dull, boring with focus on design over everything else. There are literally millions of websites like this.

I have been asked to build websites for customers and before I knew better, I would build a pretty website for a company that at the time they loved.

In more recent times, when talking to those clients a couple of years after their site has been built and they want it re-designed because they are probably a bit bored of it and it is out of date.

Now is the time I ask what they want to achieve. Usually people don't really know!

I always try and point out that there are some key things that their site needs to be doing to make it worthwhile:-

- Is there site attracting a high volume of targeted traffic?
- Are they incentivising visitors and prospects to give their details so a list is being built every day?

- Are those prospects being marketed to so they turn into paying customers?
- Are those clients being channelled back to your site repeatedly so they become repeat customers?

If your website is doing any of these things, you are above average. If it is doing none of them, you need to address this NOW!

Have you heard of the phrase "above the fold" in reference to websites? If not, it relates to how newspapers present headlines on newsstands. Often the newspapers are folded over but you can still see the headline which is a deliberate tactic to draw people in so they buy the paper.

Exactly the same principle applies to websites! It is vital that you arouse the visitors interest immediately, without them having to scroll down and look for it!

How long have you got to capture the attention of a visitor to your website?

Less than 8 seconds!

Think about what could attract your attention when you go on a website....

Write a great headline that instantly interests and captivates your reader so they read on...

I see so many websites that when you look at them from the perspective of a prospective client, you don't really know where you want to look.

So going back to that 8 seconds again, if you don't make it absolutely clear what you want your visitors to your site to do, then they will use the mostly highly clicked button on an internet browser....

The back button!

Then you have lost them. Gone, disappeared and potentially never to be seen again!

So what do you need to do?

You need to decide what the ultimate action is you want visitors to take when they visit your site.

For example:

- Do you want them to contact you?
- Do you want them to sign up for a free report so you capture their details?
- Do you want them to request a telephone call back for an offer such as a consultation?
- Do you want them to place an order online?
- Do you want a survey filled in?

There is a whole range of potential possibilities here but you must decide what it is and then make it extremely clear to a new visitor so they do it.

Another clear problem on many websites is giving your visitors too many options and too much choice.

If you give people too many choices, there is a very high chance they will choose NOT to make a choice!

So then they do nothing and you've lost them!

Use a strong headline that communicates what you do in a simple and direct way.

Now this definitely applies to all forms of advertising and marketing and is a tip that the vast majority of people miss. Quite simply you must focus on what benefits you can add to your client and try and define it in one sentence. This is categorically not about you as all people read marketing literature with the view "What's in it for me?"

So many websites go straight for dull and boring images such as pictures of the company factory or offices which turns the majority of people off immediately.

So the worry is that visitors will use that most commonly clicked button on the internet, the back button so you have got just a couple of seconds to grab your prospects attention.

It is so important to establish some great headlines that you can use on all your marketing materials, sales letters and website. For me, it starts with a brainstorming session and I write down at least 20 headlines, even if they sound a bit cumbersome and a bit clunky, often, with a bit of work, they can develop into something really good.

Be patient. Sometimes it's good to spend some time on your headlines, fine tune them to as close as you think and then go and have a coffee or do something else. When you revisit them, it can be amazing how sometimes one or two just click and work.

Now there's an interesting point. It is really good practice to test your headlines and what gives you best response.

Beauty is in the eye of the beholder and you may find what you felt was the best headline on a sales letter was actually the weakest in terms of response and something you felt wasn't your best work ever gives you a fantastic response!

Headlines are like an even shorter elevator pitch.

I assume you've heard that phrase before. So imagine you haven't got someone face to face in a lift and you have sent them a sales letter that arrives in the post along with a dozen other pieces of mail.

When your letter is opened and they very quickly twig that you're trying to flog your products or services, you have seconds to grab their attention. So make it good!

This principle applies to websites and all other marketing literature. What is also interesting, when you find something that works really well in the written word, you can even test a version of it as the spoken word too.

So clearly it will have to be worded differently, but what you are looking for is the raw nerve that you can hit with your clients and prospects, the key thing that makes them respond. We'll talk more about customers' pain later in the book, but if you can define what motivates your customers to buy, then this is the foundation for your headline. There is one way to find this out..... Ask!!

Why make it hard for people to work it out for themselves?

So many businesses have what is in effect a very lazy or presumptuous approach in that they let customers try and work out for themselves what is the benefit of your product and services. Now this is kind of dangerous as everyone can interpret messages in different ways, kind of like Chinese whispers!

Simply tell your customers in a clear and concise way. Now boring statements like "we've been in business for 20 years" is not what I'm talking about. So what, good for you but that's adding no value to your customer or prospects!

An immediate example is if you've read thus far, the title of this book hooked you in...

From Ordinary to Extraordinary

In 12 months

Marketing Guide for Small Business Owners

*Simple steps guaranteed to transform your business from
just ticking over to a
Lead Generating
Money Making Machine!*

Now I am not trying to hoodwink and fool my clients and prospects. We all have benefits and value in some way for our clients in our business or we wouldn't be in business.

The key is to define them, thinking from the perspective of people who want your product and services.

Use these tactics on your website to make headlines grab the visitor and draw them in.

Benefits, benefits, benefits!

Throughout your online marketing and offline marketing literature you need to think about every benefit your business gives its clients.

Think about what your prospects would need to believe and understand what would make what you're selling a no brainer!

Again, a benefit is not how good your team are or the quality of your equipment or how your widgets are the best money can buy... these are all features. If you look at the marketing literature and websites of the vast majority of Small Businesses, you will find them packed with features like these as well as messages from the Managing Director, Chairman or whatever the owner wants to call himself, that re-iterate the same features.

This also leads on to another subject of adding personality to your business that I will talk about later in this book.

Often statements are from the business generally – who ever speaks to a business?

A business cannot speak!

What actually is a "business". In real terms, a business is just a registered number at Companies House! A business can be a dormant name, waiting for someone to do something with it, or it can be a vibrant, dynamic thing. It is what is behind the business that is important... and that is actual human beings!

Wow what a concept!!

Quite frankly, none of us really care that much about the business we are buying from; we care about ourselves and our own current need.

OK, I do know many of us do care about the types of suppliers we use and make sure they are genuine, fair, ethical etc. but once we have judged a business on our values, ultimately we use their products and services to satisfy our own needs.

Generally, if we are looking for a particular product or service, it is because we have a need or requirement, which partially dependent on what your business provides, generally is referred to as the "Customers Pain".

If we can quickly, clearly and concisely define how we can solve this pain, and then we are making great tracks towards making a sale.

So many companies miss this point entirely so if you can harness this really powerful point then you will immediately have a head start. Why leave it up to your customer to work it out for themselves? If you are doing this, then you are leaving it open to interpretation and the real benefits of your products and services may get missed by your prospects and there is a real danger you will lose a sale.

Let's put this into an actual context.

What do builders do? Ok, if they are a residential builder, they build houses. But think about what the end result is. Do you sit in your house thinking about what lovely roof tiles you have? Do you lie in bed at night and think lovingly about how great the wiring and plastering is in your house.... Please note, if you do this you probably need to get a life!

Back to the serious point, what builders do is create *homes*, not buildings. Homes, that hold memories for you and where you spend large amounts of valuable time with your friends and family. Your home is where you are all together, through good times and bad creating memories. They create an absolutely fundamental part of people's lives.

Now how many builders deliver marketing messages that focus on this? Imagine if you are looking for a builder and you found one that talks about building memories. Or on the other hand, if you found a number of builders and if one of them talked consistently about how they help you through a process to building the home of their dreams. How they make it easy for you by taking the worries away and focus on the end result of a dream home.

Kind of takes the money and cost part of it out of the equation. I'm not saying you would necessarily pay any amount to use this builder but you would certainly seriously consider a builder who used this approach higher than the other options who do not even mention it and just tell you they've been in business 20 years!

So think about what it is your customers are ultimately looking to achieve and the benefit they gain to buying from you. Find what it is that eases their pain and focus on this.

Some people in more of the luxury, top end market miss the point here about pain when they are selling items that are not necessities and think that there can't be any pain when you don't really need it.

But anything that people buy has a connotation of easing customer pain. People buy luxury items to make themselves feel better. People use accountants to do their books and file their accounts and calculate their tax as the pain of not doing it is probably disastrous and expensive!

Other people go to Spa's or luxury weekend breaks as they are tired and stressed or just want to make themselves feel better and spend time with their loved ones. All of this relates to a form of pain.

Make sure you solve your customers pain and communicate how you do this to as many of your target prospects as possible!

Ordering online

If you own an online business where you want customers to buy online it is critical that the ordering process is as simple as possible.

I always have a simple way of testing my sites and that is to try and look at it as if I have never been online before and it is my first time placing an order.

It sounds corny but if you take the approach that if it is easy for an online newbie to do it, you are doing something right!

Make your payment process as simple as possible and make sure you can accept all major forms of online payment so that doesn't stop your buyers from bailing out at the last moment.

Upsell and Cross Sell

If you can tempt a new prospect to buy your irresistible offer, it is then a big opportunity to tempt them to buy other products at the same time.

This is relevant when selling offline too but the beauty of doing it online is the fact you can automate it and you won't have a sales person forgetting to ask the customer if they want to buy other items!

If you have other products that go hand in hand with the product your customer is buying, then it's a prime opportunity to give extra value and increase the items in the transaction.

Perhaps you can offer bundled deals or a discount on other products. Remember it's far easier to sell to an existing customer or someone who has made that buying decision than it is to find new customers. So thing this through and most importantly test different offers to see what words best.

How do I build my List?

Well as the "money is in the list" your website is the primary way of building up a loyal following of prospects that you can then implement a strategy to build a relationship with.

So what's the quickest way of doing this?

You need to incentivise your prospects to give you their details by offering them something of real value to them.

Now by value, I am not talking about discounts or money off or free products. The best way of doing this is by giving away some information and if you package this up as a Free Special Report that you can email your prospect when they give you their name and email address, it works brilliantly well.

A Free report must be written in a way that is not a sales brochure, but some information that is directly relevant to what your business does, or maybe what a particular product or service does.

If it is a blatant sales and advertising attempt, it will not work as people can very quickly see this. The report must have credibility, it must be valuable to your prospects and it must be perceived as real value to your prospect.

The advantage of a great report is it shows you and your business to have some real expertise. You need to aim to be seen as the expert in your field and this builds trust with your prospects.

So it's a winner in two ways. You have captured your prospects details and you have set yourself as a credible expert in your industry.

How do you structure a Free Report?

You do need to use strong headlines that as usual capture your readers' attention quickly.... Yep, same old story but it's true!

It is important to get across that you understand the issues and the problems that they face with regard to the subject of the report.

If you can quickly show that you can really get to the crux of the matter and you can empathise their issues and frustrations, you will quickly capture attention.

Whatever you decide to call your report, make sure it quickly gives people the relevant information that helps them solve the problem you are addressing for them and more importantly, make sure that the answers revolve around the product or service that you sell!

So, for example, here are some ideal sample titles you can adapt to your business:-

- The 19 mistakes _____ make when they are trying to _____ and how YOU can overcome them in 3 easy steps
- The 7 secret steps every _____ must know before buying _____

- The 29 Top Tips on how to grow your business by
 ____ in 60 days or less

It is well worth considering using headlines that focus on what people could be losing out on if there are not doing XYZ because there is a much stronger motivation in fear.

Fear is without doubt a strong driving force and I recommend you think of a list of potential headlines that focus on this powerful strategy and remember the headline is what will get people to read further.

The report needs to make the answer look straight forward and systematic and make it really clear what action needs to be taken. But importantly, you do not give away exactly how you may solve this problem but emphasise that you can solve it.

Now you need to back this up.

Simple way to do this is case studies and testimonials showing how you have resolved this issue for others.

Like many forms of copywriting, make the report conversational, use short sentences and short paragraphs so it's very easy to read. Make sure you get across your credibility and expertise.

Then you finish the report with a great offer and a direct call to action. Because you have set out your understanding of the problems they face, you have detailed how you resolve it and how you have done this for others, and your prospect will be significantly more receptive to an irresistible offer!

It is important you have it professionally designed so it looks great, you include good images and graphics if this is relevant to your business and include information on you and how they can easily contact you to take you up on your offer!

So where do you put the sign up to the report?

There are two approaches that you need to consider here. The first is what is known as a "squeeze page" or a "lead page".

This is a simple, one page website that single function is to offer this report and back up why your prospect needs to sign up and download it.

It definitely does not have a load of tabs and other pages with "About Us" and a load of product or service information pages.

You do not want people browsing, getting some snippets of information that they think is sufficient and then leaving the site.

You need to aim to get a high proportion of visitors to sign up for your report so you capture their details.

Your web designer should understand this system if you have no technical awareness of this, but your autoresponder system will be able to create some code to embed into your squeeze page so all sign ups will automatically go into a database and your report can be sent to them automatically.

I recommend systems like aWeber, Marcatushq.com, Infusion Soft, MailChimp but there are a number of different options. I use Marcatushq.com as it is simple and straight forward to use which is ideal whereas some systems are over complicated for most peoples' requirements.

You can use on and offline marketing to promote this page. So maybe email marketing or banner advertising could be used and when your prospect clicks onto this link, it takes them directly to your squeeze page.

If you use a simple domain name for the squeeze page such as www.yourfreereportname.com so you don't use the main domain for your site.

This will help ensure people are not browsing around your site distracting them from signing up.

To encourage your prospects to sign up, there is a trade off between how much information you ask from them. If you are insisting on full name, address, email, website, telephone number and so forth, you are going to deter a lot of potential sign ups.

So, good practice is to make it compulsory to just ask for their name and email address.

If you balance this with giving a physical product such as a book or a hard copy of the report, then obviously you can ask for their address details.

Don't forget that email is a highly acceptable form of communication so I would suggest this is the best option initially.

Privacy is paramount!

I don't know for sure about you, but I don't like spam! I would also put money that your prospects don't want to be spammed either!

So I suggest you use a statement similar to this to reassure people:-

> **PRIVACY GUARANTEE:** *Your information is 100% safe and will never be sold or rented. (Your company name) will keep in touch by email and post. If you've had enough, it's easy to unsubscribe. We'll shed a tear but won't bother you... promise.*

Once they have signed up, the information will go directly into your autoresponder system which must be set up to send your report out automatically and also send up a follow up sequence to start building a relationship with your prospect.

Just owning this database alone will not make you rich! You need to be regularly offering high quality information to them so you become a trusted figure and if they are in a position to buy a product or service your business sells, it is your name that is paramount in their mind.

Please don't make a mistake that many people do and that is to send a couple of emails out and then kind of let it drop off to nothing very quickly.

Not everyone will buy straightaway. So don't give up on them and be the company of choice when they are ready. This could take days, weeks or months to happen.

Persistence is key!

CHAPTER FOUR:

Do my customers know who I am?

Now of course people buy products and services because they need them and there is a chance they will shop around in some way to find a company that can provide what they want.

People often go with a choice that makes them feel comfortable and in effect go with a low risk option more often than not.

We all know the phrase better the devil you know. Well sometimes we have to try and instigate that feeling of trust.

So how do you try and make sure that you have more people find out about your business and in a way where they feel comfortable?

We ask people who know and like what we do to tell others... not rocket science is it!

Think about this scenario:

A good friend calls you up and says they have a friend who is starting a business selling widgets, let's call him Mr X and as your friend knows you regularly buy widgets, as a favour to help Mr X out would you talk to him about the possibility of buying them from this new business?

Well if it was me and the phone call was from a friend I trusted and he has always helped me out in the past, it would really not be a problem to go on their recommendation to try out Mr X's new business.

Reason being, there is a strong relationship and trust.

So, the opposing scenario is you receive a cold call from Mr X who tells you he is starting a widget business and he asks you to buy his widgets and he will give you a great deal.

Now widgets are vital to your business and you need a reliable supplier. You have no idea who Mr X is and you would rather play it safe and stick to the widget supplier you know and trust. So the chances are Mr X loses out.

OK, so wouldn't it be ideal for our friends and good acquaintances to be recommending us to other friends all day long? We can try and make this happen as often as possible, but let's get real!

This is probably going to only happen a certain number of times and I talk in a later chapter about how we endeavour to make this happen because when it does, it's great, but you probably can't build a business on the hope that this will happen.

So you need to look at other ways you can instigate a relationship and make referrals happen more often. Ultimately people buy people and the vast majority of small to medium sized businesses are faceless and hugely lacking in personality.

Richard Branson has hundreds of businesses and he is not involved with running any of them day to day, but every time one of the Virgin companies has a launch of some kind, he is everywhere doing some kind of PR stunt as well as photoshoots, interviews, you name it, he is doing it!

Now there is a very good reason that *Billionaire* Richard Branson keeps doing this.

It works!

People know him, like him and trust him! So people feel very comfortable about spending money with a Virgin company.

Now let's be realistic, most of us are not in Richard Branson's league so we have to work hard to emulate a tiny proportion of his success.

My point is, generally speaking most business owners are relatively unknown to their prospects and their websites and marketing literature often give very little personal comment or personality.

The approach of becoming a face of your business is a personal choice, but for me, when I look at using new companies and buying new products and services, whether it is sub conscious or not, I look for the people behind the name, the logo and the look of the business.

I feel much more comfortable if I can find out a bit about the owners and managers and if I relate to them it seems to put me in buying mode much quicker.

Think about how you position yourself in your business, the words you use when talking about yourself, your businesses products and services.

Why do so many people write sales copy as if it's some kind of boasting exercise when if you spoke like that in a face to face meeting you would probably sound ridiculous and never get the business!

No-one likes a show off!

Write as if you are talking and add some personality to your copy! It's easier to read when it is written in a conversational manner and when you write in this way you will naturally add your personality to your copy. You will naturally create a style of writing that is recognisable and even if you decide to bring in some professional help to write this, it is important that this style is maintained.

A really good copy writer will be able to emulate a chosen style and as long as the style you have chosen works well in your chosen field of expertise, you will have much better response than corporate speak full of the latest buzzwords!

Now as you build a personality in your business that people relate to in a positive way, as you deliver great customer service, put in simple procedures that help you generate more leads.

How do you do this quickly and easily?

It really is as simple as phoning your customers and asking them! After sales service is a task that many businesses neglect. It is a common fault that people assume that a customer is happy with the product or service you provide.

So how do you know if they are unhappy?

Possibly you won't because you will never see them again if they were dissatisfied.

An unhappy customer is an opportunity. Even a customer who is only slightly unhappy is a chance to improve your business.

Imagine if you bought a product from a business and a day later you had a phone call and they asked you some questions about your experience. If you think about the last buying experience you had and were asked to rate the experience out of 10. How many times would you give full marks?

Now this is exactly what we are looking for in this system. If you give any score other than 10 and were then asked, "So what could we do to help improve that score?" Imagine how powerful that is for the selling company if they asked all of their customers that question! An opportunity to give customers exactly what they want means one result which is continual improvement and returning customers.

This is the lifeblood of every business.

You actually want a proportion of people who are unhappy because although you can't please all the people all of the time, some of this feedback will be common to other prospects so you can use this information to capture more happy customers and meet their expectations.

So as you and your team speak to all of your customers as part of your after sales follow up procedure, you have a number of opportunities:-

1. Enquire about customer satisfaction
2. Ask how your customers rate their experience
3. Ask how that score could be improved
4. If clients are very happy, ask for a testimonial
5. If they are happy to do a testimonial ask if this can be used as part of a case study
6. Ask who they know who could also benefit from your products and services and if you can use their name when contacting their references
7. If necessary, implement a rewards scheme to incentivise more clients to refer you more often.

Now if you are a small business or have a low number of clients, it is relatively easy to implement this system. If you have a larger business with a large client base and do not have the resources to contact every single client personally by telephone, then this system can be automated online using a service like SurveyMonkey, an online survey system. (Just Google Survey Monkey and sign up, it's really easy to use).

Of course this is not as personal but it can still have the desired result if you carefully word your survey and not make it an endless number of questions that people start but quickly lose the will to live!

Sometimes an incentive helps improve the number of responses, especially if it is aimed at bringing in more referrals. Often, people liked to be asked for their help and especially if you are setting yourself apart from your competition by actually finding out what your customers think!

CHAPTER FIVE:
Show them Proof

When you are looking at making a purchase, what do you think would convince you that it is worth the money? Would a salesman who continually tells you how great it is or a series of other happy customers telling you how it benefitted them?

To me it's thinking about an actual conversation you would have with someone, either face to face or on the telephone.

No-one likes a show off or someone who just plain boasts!

If you just continually tell your propects how great you are before there is any relationship building activity, it is human nature for them to be put off you.

By boasting about how great you are, it is possible you can actually have the reverse of the desired effect!

We just don't want to hear about you, you, you!

If it is going to be difficult to build relationships by telling people directly how great you are then how do you do it?

Well, why not ask your satisfied customers to do it for you?

Basic psychology but we all believe a third party telling us about their experiences of a service, product or company than we do from the company selling it!

If a customer tells us about a company we are considering buying from, it sounds far more believable than if the company is doing it themselves.

Independent, first-hand knowledge of a positive experience is massively powerful.

It's perfectly obvious but so many businesses fail to capture and document testimonials and case studies. When you think about it, it makes such obvious sense, but it's very important to implement a strategy in your business to collect high quality, varied testimonials and using the after sales system I talked about in the last chapter is a great way of doing this consistently.

So what is a great testimonial?

When your prospects read a testimonial, they need to be able to relate to it so it needs to be relevant and talk about how your client benefited from using your product or service.

"Bill's accountancy practice was good to deal with and made my bookkeeping easy"

How does that sound? Well its ok isn't it but it's not going to cause a stampede of prospective customers is it?!

How about the following...

"Since using Bill's accountancy practice, I've not only saved myself 10 hours per week in accountancy administration which has given me more time to focus on developing a new product range, but Bill has also managed to save me 32% off my tax bill. I thoroughly recommend Bill's accountancy practice to all small business owners who want to <u>save time and money</u>"

Isn't that dramatically better? Why? Well simply because the customer talks directly about the benefits, giving detail on how Bill helped save his business time and money (something we all like to save!). It gives specific information and it also mentions what sort of client would be suitable so if you fit into that category, it almost makes it a no brainer!

So how do I get testimonials like this and what do I do with them?

Well like many things in life, if you don't ask you don't get! Speak to your satisfied customers, explain why you are asking but most importantly make it as simple as possible for them by perhaps giving examples like the one above so they get the idea.

Perhaps even offer to write the testimonial draft for them and email it to them so they can edit it or read a few out to them.

Then the most important part is to ask their permission to use their name, company and perhaps their web address, every time you quote the testimonial. You could use their picture and even better, if they are prepared to go on video with their testimonial it's extremely powerful.

Adding that personal touch gives real proof that it's real and not something that you've made up yourself.... You want your prospects to believe it and then you will have your satisfied clients doing the selling for you!

Now the beauty of continually collecting testimonials, it gives you fantastic **content** to add to your website. You may be aware that search engines love new content so if you are struggling to write new content yourself, a systematic and continuous testimonial program will give you a steady stream of content to add to your site.

This is both powerful and extremely relevant to your target reader – your prospects! It is also a good way to remind your current and past clients of what a great job you do!

CHAPTER SIX:

Feel the fear and confront it!

I'm not talking bungee jumping, the dark, sharks, watching Doctor Who from behind a cushion (oops, is that just me!) or confronting *your* personal fears!

I am talking about the fear customers and prospects feel before they buy!

So who do you think feels the fear?

Well, all of us do before we let go of any of our hard earned cash and make a purchase, especially if it's from a new supplier.

So how do we remove this fear?

Well fear is there because there is a risk and because of the unknown. What happens if I don't like it or what happens if it goes wrong / doesn't work etc?

I'm sure you have experienced this before you have taken the leap with using a new company and it is quite likely you will have on more than one occasion walked away because you were not quite sure and felt the risk was too great to commit.

It is not just the cost of the product or service we are buying from a new supplier that worries us. It is the knock on effect!

What if it is business critical and we end up getting let down? Well then that old phrase kicks in...

"Better the devil you know"

That is the worst thing you want new prospects to be saying or thinking if they are unsure about you or they way up the risk and decide it's better if they either don't buy at all, or stick to the supplier they know.

I bet you have experienced the massive frustration when you are millimetres from winning a new client but you lose it at the last hurdle when they just aren't satisfied that you are a safe enough bet.

It's a horrible feeling; trust me I've been there. Particularly harsh when you know who your competition is and you know that you can provide a better product or service but the customer is just not sure enough to go with you.

So after a failure like this, it is sometimes a chance to go back to the drawing board and decided what to do next.

- How can we make our prospects feel better about using us?
- How can we eliminate the competition?
- How can we make the buying decision much easier and quicker for new customers?

We have to overcome the fear and we have to prove that it is a no brainer decision. We need to remove the risk and actually give them a choice that is so easy, it happens quickly.

So how do we confront this fear that our clients feel and how do we make steps to remove it?

*In a word...*Guarantees.

If you offer an absolute failsafe guarantee, that removes all the risk the customer will feel protected and far more likely to buy from you.

Money back guarantees are extremely powerful but there are other ways of doing it such as offering free replacements for a period of time, or a 100% satisfaction guarantee so your customer knows you will not take their money and disappear but you will stick around long enough to make sure they are happy.

It's vitally important that your guarantee is extremely strong and stands out from the norm in your industry. It must be so powerful people take note of it and it has an impact. Many business people feel nervous that potentially unscrupulous customers may take advantage but you will be amazed how a fantastic guarantee increases your sales and this far outweighs the odd person who tries to take advantage.

The beauty of introducing a new, powerful guarantee is you can use it as a marketing tool and really promote it to all your customers and prospects to invigorate your business. You need to make it a real statement so it's really bold and a key feature in all your marketing literature and on your website.

Don't hide it away hoping no-one will take advantage of it, but be proud of it. Don't just say it's a 100% Guarantee but similarly to your testimonials, really dramatise it so it has impact...

Use Bill's accountancy practice with Total Peace of Mind. You are covered by our 100% Risk Free Satisfaction Guarantee

If you are not completely satisfied with our accountancy service we will work Free of charge to rectify any problem for up to 30 days until you are happy, or your money back!

Now don't you think that has more impact? If you were contemplating using a new accountant and had the option of Bill's accountancy practice or one of his competitors, this statement would help you make a decision.

Of course most businesses will be open to some form of negotiation, goodwill and legal obligation if their product or service is sub-standard, but the difference is, if you are bold enough to state it clearly and concisely it can be used as an extremely powerful marketing tool and should be used on every piece of marketing literature and _especially_ on your website as many new clients use the internet to do their research before buying.

Be Pro-active to remove your customers fear without them even knowing it. Make it an absolute no-brainer for them so the decision to purchase is completely obvious and without any risk on their part.

We have already talked about focussing on benefits so this is paramount in helping your customers subconsciously think about the positives.

Now, with a failsafe, cast iron guarantee, it removes the risk and the negatives that they may have had.... And you have massively improved the chances of making a sale!

CHAPTER SEVEN:

Who is visiting your website?

So many websites for SME's are basically online brochures. They add very little value and have all the typical symptoms of failing websites as they purely talk about themselves. You know the type of thing you get about how passionate they are about their work, how they "pride themselves in great customer service" etc etc.

All extremely dull and I bet you will have skipped through loads of websites in the past that are instantly forgettable. Now, think back to your website. I know our own websites hold very personal feelings and we are often proud of the way they look and spent hours mulling over the copy for your web designer to use.

But, apply some of the detail I've talked about in this report. How often do you talk about the benefits to the customer and the value you add to them and how your product and service will improve their life in some way?

Now to the question of who is visiting your website? I like to use a very simple comparison story here to demonstrate how ridiculous most websites are when you think about it.

Ok, so you commission my business PrintRepublic.co.uk to design and print a 1000 lovely full colour, laminated, high quality brochures for you. We deliver them to your office and you open the boxes and feel full of pride about how lovely they are.

So the next morning, you and a couple of members of your team wander down to your local high street and you start handing them out to passers-by who happily take one as they then go about their day to day business.

In a few hours you've managed to hand out all 1000 and you trot happily back to your office and wait for the phone to ring..... but nothing happens. So the next day you phone me up, slightly bewildered as to where you went wrong.

So I ask you a couple of questions about what you did and you explain how you went to the high street, handed them out to people who all seemed impressed and commented on what a lovely brochure it was and yes they did occasionally have a need for the widgets that you sell. I then asked you a question that made the end of the phone go silent... "So who are the people you gave the brochures out to and how are you going to follow them up?"

So here's the problem with most websites for SME's. Who on earth are the people who are visiting your website that you paid a small fortune for, much like those lovely brochures we designed and printed for you?

What's the solution then?

The answer is what is known as "Permission Marketing"

This is the process of gaining permission from your target prospects to build a relationship with them. It is a process and concept missed by so many businesses that it's scary. At the same time, being the eternal optimist, I see it as a monumental opportunity to make huge headway in your business is you implement this strategy as there is every chance many of your competitors are not doing this!

If you have built a brand and an image that your prospects relate to and is representative of the products and services your business sells, you are then focussing on the benefits to your customers, if you have a list that you develop and nurture by building a relationship, you will naturally create trust. People will start to relate to you and if they do that, you will start to become much more successful.

So how do you build a list?

Well you need to incentivise as many of the visitors of your site to give you their information. You may have heard the saying "the money is in the list". If you are building a strong, up to date and growing list of prospects and buyers you are building value in your business.

If you have a database that you build a relationship with, you have a far greater chance of selling to those people.

The amount of information you need is dependent on what you give away and the nature of the business you are in, but as a minimum you want their email address, but up to their name, postal address, telephone and email address are possible. The more you ask for is a trade off on what you give them, but a word or warning, as a general rule, the more information you ask for, the lower the response rate.

If you are in a business that sells very high value items and you may only want a handful of customers a month and you want very targeted buyers, then this is ok buy my guess most businesses need a reasonable amount of prospects so I would say a name and email address would be a great start.

What do I give for Free to incentivise my prospects?

Again, dependent on the business and industry sector you are in determines this, but it could be anything from a FREE report on how your product and service can benefit them, to maybe a sample of your products, a try before you buy offer, there are loads of ways of doing this so you need to think this through.

At PrintRepublic we have used an extremely successful campaign of giving away FREE Business cards to new clients. It has worked as a double whammy as we are showing new clients the quality of our printing, but by doing so we are giving them a product they can use and adds value to them immediately. If you can offer a win-win scenario like this it often has fantastic results and we are building a list of thousands that is growing every single day of the week.

How do I capture the prospects details?

In a very prominent part of your homepage, you need a clear box stating your proposed offer and have a sign up form. It is so important that you make it clear that you need people to fill in their details to get their FREE gift. There is a simple way of doing this... Tell them!

Give visitors to your site one clear call to action and instruct them in what to do. Tell people to do it there and then. Do not give loads of different options. Make a clear statement of intent that you want them to put their information into the simple form now and the benefit of doing so. Also make it clear that you will not spam them or sell their details on to anyone else. People will sign up as one of the best words to use in marketing is "free"!

To capture the leads in the sign up box, you will need to have an account with an email service such as MarcatusMail, InfusionSoft or Aweber (or a number of other options), so the data goes straight into a database and you can then set up a series of automatically sent out follow up emails.

At PrintRepublic we use MarcatusMail as this is a fantastic solution that is easy to use and we can help you set up this account, create a personalised email template and integrate it into your website so don't get too scared... help is on hand!

If you get a chance to read a book called InBox Gold, written by Andy Gooday who runs Marcatus, do so. It gives you a great guide on how to maximise what you do with e-marketing.

A great series of follow up emails is vital as not everyone is ready to buy immediately so it is of paramount importance you remain fresh in their minds so when they are in buying mode, they immediately think of you.

It is estimated that you need to spend an average of 7 hours building a relationship with prospective customers before they are ready to buy. Now this is across any form of communication platform you have with a customer.

So it could be the time they spend on your website, reading your blog and emails, looking at your marketing literature, telephone calls and of course face to face.

So again, it brings up the point of consistency across every way in which you communicate. If you employ a sales team plus anyone who speaks to customers either face to face or on the telephone, it shows how if they are well briefed and singing off the same hymn sheet, it really focuses the message you want to get across.

In the same way as not making your marketing messages clear and concise for your clients when they go onto your website or read your marketing literature, do not leave it up to your team to individually think up their own way of selling, trying their own promotions and quite simply watering down your sales effort!

In a highly competitive world where we are all bombarded with literally thousands of marketing messages every single day, make sure yours are managed, targeted and as effective as possible!

CHAPTER EIGHT:

Make sure everything is singing from the same hymn sheet!

Let's imagine you have a team of sales people who are on the telephone talking to customers and out in the field visiting new and existing customers on a daily basis.

Not an unusual scenario I know, but now let's imagine them all acting completely independently and adding their own ideas on what to sell, how much to sell it for and just as importantly who they are targeting.

I also know this is not hugely uncommon when sales teams do not have strict control and some guidelines as to what they should or should not be doing, but I think you would agree that when companies let this scenario happen it is largely ineffective and a recipe for disaster.

I think we would also be quite quick to say that this wouldn't happen in our business and we would have regular updates and meeting to ensure our sales team are consistent and controlled in an effective way.

OK, so having agreed that, is the marketing literature, websites etc that you put into the marketplace being dealt with in the same way?

So if you are a new business or have re-branded, or you already have a logo and an image for your business that has been created by a design agency... or a freelancer.... or in-house.... or by yourself.... Well, however it was created, you want it to be consistent across every touchpoint of your business – website, business cards, leaflets, flyers, brochures, signage etc

The logo is just the starting point. The biggest issue facing many small business owners is what and how to tell their prospects and customers about their products and services.

There is a well-known phrase that is very apt...

"If you don't tell, you don't sell!"

So you have to make sure you continually tell your customers what you do. How many times have you met with a client who in casual conversation mentions that they have hired a new supplier to do something that you could have easily have delivered for them?

How frustrating is this?

Especially when you have mentioned that you provide that product or service to them in the past! This really emphasises my next point

Customers only listen to you when they have a direct requirement for your product or service.

Often businesses send clients a new juicy brochure which details their whole portfolio of products and services. More often than not nowadays, all of that information is on your website. But do you realistically think your new and old customers will know that website as intimately as you?

Two hopes of this – "Bob" and "No"!!

We are only interested about that product or service as and when we are in buying mode. Even if we glance through a website or brochure and see something that could be relevant, the chances of remembering it are often slim and when another company happens to be communicating a marketing message whilst you are ready to buy, it is highly likely that you will use them as you may not .

How do we minimise this risk?

It used to be said that you need 7 pieces of communication with a prospect for them to remember your names, brand, product or service. This is now significantly higher. We are all bombarded with literally thousands of marketing messages every day so the knock on effect is we become a little immune and get a kind of "advertising blindness"

So if we need to be communicating dozens and dozens of times with both clients and prospects, my original point regarding consistency is vital.

We have already spoken about benefits and not "brand" advertising. So we have to think carefully about this and ensure our marketing communications have a series of common traits that are recognisable.

Consistency across all Marketing Channels

Let's go back a stage then. You have your logo, you need a website, marketing literature and promotional flyers, emarketing, signage.

You also have a day job to organise! Yep I know, this kind of stuff seems to take forever to sort! Don't forget to not take your finger off the pulse of your business either!

So my guess, busy business people like you need a little help. Getting logos sorted, designing and building websites, continually design content for flyers, direct mail, websites, emailers, blogs etc. takes time and it needs co-ordinating.

At PrintRepublic, our customers have told us that running a small business and co-ordinating all of this stuff is very much akin to that juggling thing! Keep all the balls in the air and if you drop the marketing one, business suffers.... Drop the customer service one.... business suffers!

Integrated marketing ensures your customers have clarity about what you do, consistently reminds them when they are not in buying mode, but still reminds them when they are!

CHAPTER NINE:

Use every media possible to get your message across

So how many emails do you get on an average working day? If your inbox is anything like mine it's too many!

Ok, so how many do you read and how many do you take action on?

Again, if an email has a good subject and when I open it, it very quickly grabs my attention I will probably ready some or all of it.

If it happens by chance to be promoting or selling something that by pure luck is what I am looking for at that moment in time, then of course I will open it and take the appropriate action which is often signing up for a seminar, requesting more information and even more occasionally buying something there and then!

If I think it could be of interest at a later date, I keep it... for a while and then when I am making some space in my inbox I delete it. All the rest, I probably just delete!

I guess you are much the same. Unless we are specifically looking for that product or service at that moment in time we tend to not respond.

Email open rates are reducing because in my view we are all just a little bit punch drunk from receiving them incessantly.

So, one trend that is reversing is the improvement in the response rate from direct mail. In the last decade, direct mail has gone from a significantly successful media to a potentially highly costly marketing method, especially if it fails to work!

We have all heard of email spam but that is the same principle that was adopted by companies running direct mail campaigns under the assumption that there is a scatter gun approach but if some of the mud sticks, it will potentially pay off!

If you buy a database of 100's, 1000's or as we ran for some clients, literally in the millions, there is always a massive proportion who will not buy off you if you were the last company in the world! Nothing personal, just that they have no interest or need in what you offer and as direct mail was, and to an extent is, a numbers game, you will always be hitting some prospects that are basically a waste of time and money to your business. It is very hard to know who they are if they just delete your email or chuck your direct mail piece in the bin!

But marketers are today getting smarter and the way in which databases are used is much more targeted and effective!

Let's start at the beginning and the foundation of any email or direct mail campaign....

The database!

As I have already spoken about building your own list is absolutely the best approach to take, I cannot recommend this strategy enough. It's absolutely crucial to build your own database, no matter what industry you are in. However it can also be an option to consider to ramp up your marketing activity quicker by buying a database.

When buying a list of a list broker, you need to be very selective and negotiate hard. Ideally, you want a random selection of the data to test... make sure it is random otherwise some unscrupulous list brokers will send you some of the most recent and fresh data that will potentially give you the best returns so you buy, only to find the rest of the list is a little overworked and not as responsive!

Stating an obvious point but one that is not considered carefully enough by business owners in my view is who the database contacts actually are. I can't emphasise enough how you need to really think about who you are targeting. Also, not just assuming who you are targeting are people who really want your products and services but actually testing and analysing to make sure.

If you have a current database you need to really look at the profiles of the people or companies on it. If you are targeting businesses then the type and size of business, location and the job titles of the people within that business is all crucial information.

If you are starting from scratch, you need to test any list by asking for some sample data before you commit to buying.

So purchased lists can be effective although I have known campaigns I have run for my business and also for clients where campaigns have bombed! This is why testing is so vital so you can try and eliminate the cause and increase responsiveness in future.

There are always a number of factors that can make or break a direct mail campaign.

1. The database
2. The creative (i.e. the actual design of the mailpiece)
3. The offer

If any of these factors are not at least half right, then you will not get good results. There is a common with many business owners when direct mail campaigns fail to give the desired result. They give up!

Just like that. One attempt and if it doesn't work you can hear the words now.

"Yep, I tried Direct Mail, rubbish, it doesn't work!"

If you recall what I said about testing, if you don't learn something about each marketing activity, you are wasting your time. You must test and learn with everything you do, so if you try direct mail just once you may as well not bother.

But if you try it more than once, make sure you do not start from scratch. You must only change one of the 3 key factors otherwise how are you going to learn anything?

Often the first thing to change is the content and more specifically the offer. You almost definitely do not want to scrap the database because you will be starting from complete scratch if you do this and mail a whole new list.

Integrated Campaigns

So what does this little buzz phrase mean? Well if we think about the end result, we want as much as response as possible from any campaign, that goes without saying.

Now different people respond to different forms of communication. I bet you know some people, maybe yourself, who are addicted to the Blackberry or whatever smart phone they use. Email is being checked continuously wherever they are.

I also know a few people who have really basic mobile phones that look like they came out of the ark and all they are interested in doing is making phone calls (wow, what a weird, antiquated idea!) whereas other people may have the latest gadget but they never turn the bloody thing on!

So do you think the same means of communication will work equally well for all three types? Of course not! There are also a variety of other factors relevant to response such as timing and whether your prospect is ready to buy, but it is often impossible to really know every detail for this.

So we have to use a variety of different media to try and ring the individual bell of each person on your list.

So this is where you need to look at running integrated campaigns that use media that will cover the personal requirements across the spectrum of your list.

So a phased approach needs to be rolled out which includes email marketing, direct mail and a telesales follow up.

Generally speaking there is not necessarily a specific order in which you do email and direct mail but I suggest you test this for your list and your specific market, but I recommend you add a telesales follow up after carrying out the first 2 operations.

I don't know about you but I find cold calling incredibly hard to do and often it feels like pushing water uphill.

Why not try and make it easier for you and your team by warming up all your leads and raising awareness by sending out a carefully planned email and direct mail follow up. Think about the ideas in previous chapters about focussing on your customers' pain and highlighting benefits, along with an engaging and highly attractive time sensitive offer.

Why put a time limit on your offer?

You must create some urgency and a direct call to action. Simply tell your prospects what to do and it is imperative you do not give too much choice.

If you give people tonnes of choice, it is highly likely they will deliberate, um and aah and ultimately choose NOT to make a choice!

So a direct "Call to Action" explaining the simple steps to placing an order and telling the prospects when to do it (i.e. Now!) so they do not lose the amazing opportunity you are offering!

CHAPTER TEN:

If you don't tell you don't sell

If you have built a database of clients and prospects then is it the case that all you have to do is sit back and count the money and watch as the sales go through the roof?

Wouldn't it be lovely if that was it!

Sadly, unless you have the most in demand, trendy and well known gizmo or gadget that the world is clamouring to get their hands on, (which is probably a little unlikely!) then it is not going to be as simple as that!

You may see a process here of tasks and skills that are like building blocks in the marketing plan. As each part of the process fits together you can put the next process in place.

So, you are building profiles of buying patterns, you have a list that is being built but it is essential that the communications you put in place carry on cementing your relationship with your clients.

If you don't tell you don't sell.

If you are not continually re-enforcing your brand awareness, your marketing messages and offering value to your customers (all at the same time!) then you realise how fickle people can be!

If you are not talking to your customers then your competitors are!

When your customer is ready to buy, that is when you sell to them. That is relatively easy if you sell a product or service on some form of timed contract as in a period of time before the end of the contract you can offer an incentive to renew it.

But this is not relevant to most businesses. So how do you know when they are ready? You can look at buying patterns and if you have seasonal products then again it is quite easy.

Simply put, for a lot of businesses, you do not know when your clients and prospects are in buying mode.

So, show them some love! Build relationships often and regularly. If you are in the forefront of your mind when they are ready to buy, then the chances are you will get the sale.

It's like any relationship. You must show interest in the other party, take time to understand what they want and show them you care.

Sometimes, you can just phone up your customers and thank them for giving you business. Simple as that! Don't sell them anything, just tell them you are pleased that they chose your business and that it's people like them that make the effort all worthwhile.

Imagine how you would feel if you got a phone call like that from one of your suppliers?

Amazingly powerful!

If you have a business that has a large volume of customers and it is just not feasible for you to phone them all, then write a letter. Make it personal and do NOT try and sell them anything - kind of defeats the point!

Focus on the best 20%

Have you heard of Pareto's Principle?

Vilfredo Pareto observed in 1906 that 20%of the Italian people owned 80% of the countries accumulated wealth.

In a business context it relates to the common fact that 20% of the effort generates 80% of the results.

It is extremely likely that this is relevant to your business in terms of your sales versus your customers. It is probable that a percentage of customers in the region of 20% that gives you something like 80% of your sales.

So it is important you focus each part of those 2 sectors in a different way.

Keep the 20% of customers as close to you as possible and keep in front of them in every sense, as often as possible.

Write to them, send emails, call them, visit them. Make sure you know what is going on in their business.

For the 80% you need to think how you can bring more of them up to becoming large clients. Incentivise them and find out what it is they are looking for.

Here is one tactic that works particularly well.

Call a selection of your clients and ask the following question...

"...is there anything that you have a requirement for that we currently don't provide you?"

Then shut up and listen. Find out what problems they have and what they have a burning desire for you to solve.

This is amazingly powerful and is worth putting in place a timed schedule to regularly do with this a selection of your best customers.

CHAPTER ELEVEN:

No Marketing Budget to Unlimited Budget

So if you look at your finances and try and workout how much you want to spend on marketing, do you have enough money in the pot to do what you want to do?

What is the classic action that so many companies take when times get a little tough? They start looking at areas where they can cut back, pull in the strings and keep things tight, hoping to ride out the recession.

There is one area where you really shouldn't be cutting back if you need more customers and you need more sales...

Marketing!

There is often no tangible result for marketing budget when people focus on "raising awareness" and "building the brand", classic mistakes discussed in earlier chapters. So if you do or don't advertise in your trade journal, or send a direct mail campaign that has traditionally generated minimal response, the only upside of doing nothing is you save some money.

You still haven't generated any SALES!

When sales are declining, it is perfectly logical to most people that you increase marketing spend and focus completely on sales and marketing but it is also clear that many people in charge of budgets decide to become slightly illogical and cut back on any marketing and focus on saving money!

This is clearly because if you do not know what you are doing and you are not measuring the response you are generating from every piece of marketing you do, you haven't got a clue whether it's working or not!

Now let's go back one stage. Think about your current clients and start to analyse the numbers you have on these clients.

- How much are they spending with you per month, per year?
- On average, how long do you keep a customer for?
- What is the average margin you make on an average customer?
- What is the Lifetime Value of an average client?

So if you can work out how much an average customer generates in revenue for you, you can start to make decisions about how much you are prepared to PAY to win more customers!

So what do I mean by paying for customers?

So let's look at some numbers to give you a clear idea about how this works.

- An average client spends £250 per order
- An average client spends £1000 per year
- They stay with you for an average of 3 years
- Your average margin is 25% which is £250 per annum
- The Lifetime Value is £3000

So how do we get more of these clients?

Let's look at your marketing activity. You spend £500 on a marketing campaign that generates 10 Leads.

Out of your 10 Leads you convert 20% which is 2 New Customers.

So each new customer has cost you £250. Wow, you start to worry that you have over spent because one order is on average only £250 so that campaign has not made you any profit!

Well like many things in business, now is when you have to think about the long game and definitely NOT the short game.

So you only have £500 of orders today against a spend of £500 but the most important thing you know when you have thought carefully about your customers and you know exactly what they are doing is that the average client will spend £3000 over 3 years!

Surely now you can see that actually this was a highly successful campaign.

You also do not know yet, but some of the other non-buying leads may also turn into customers but at a later date!

So, on this basis, what is your marketing budget? Well exactly how many customers do you want and by how much do you want to grow your business?

Now you don't really need to set a marketing budget because in theory it is unlimited because for every £500 you spend on marketing, you can generate 2 clients spending £1000 per annum over 3 years.

So you now just multiply!

Now I know this is a simplified model and I will not pretend that you have to test and measure all of your marketing to continually improve it, you keep following up leads that do not convert and you continually endeavour to keep new leads dropping into your marketing system, but if you have a complete handle on your numbers, you know exactly what your return on investment is and you can look at how much you want to grow your business with some really knowledge and analysis.

CHAPTER TWELVE:
Raise your profile

I have talked about hugely well known entrepreneurs in this book such as Richard Branson and it seems business is becoming far more prominent in the media with TV programmes such as Dragon's Den and The Apprentice.

To me, this is fantastic as I see so many young people who watch these programmes, start to aspire and think about setting up their own businesses.

That entrepreneurial spirit is what really drives our economy forward. If we can get more people starting businesses, innovating and building great businesses, that can only be great news for all of us.

Now with the increase in well known business people becoming media characters, it does highlight the potential for all business owners to start thinking about what they can do themselves.

In this age, more than ever before, it is much easier to raise your own profile far higher and to a far greater audience, much quicker than ever.

Why should I raise my profile?

Think back to the points I have made in this book about things like people buying people and the sterile image of so many businesses. How do you think you can set yourself apart?

If people buy people, start to think why it should be you that your prospects choose, rather than your competitors.

What is different about your business?

Well there is one thing your business has got that your competitors have not.

YOU!

So don't hide yourself away and let your business just be another name on the list of thousands of faceless businesses. Get yourself out of your comfort zone and shout about yourself and your business from the rooftops!

Many people are quite nervous to do this. But why fade into the background when you have a chance to really make a difference to your business and ultimately to your life when you can enjoy the fruits of your success.

The thing is, NOW is the time to take the opportunity to compete with other local business, national and international business.

There has never... EVER been more opportunity at any time to compete with Multi National businesses with immense budgets as well as the countless other competitors you may have.

How?

Simple. It is the power of the internet and more specifically Social Media.

So how are you embracing Social Media?

Are you still keeping it at arm's length?

Do you see it as a load of rubbish for kids, students, people who want to waste time on the internet contacting "friends" they have never actually met?

Well let me tell you something here and now. It is Social Media that is creating the biggest opportunity for us in our businesses we may ever see!

Social Media is just for kids' right?

Now my view was originally a very negative one on Social Media. I really did think it was a huge waste of time and was really only to have a look at in the evenings, to catch up with a few old friends and share silly stories or pictures across the internet.

At first, I just didn't get Twitter.

I heard it spoken about on the radio by a BBC Radio 5 DJ, Richard Bacon and when I started to look at it, I just thought it was a joke.

I didn't get it at all! My first impression was what an earth can you say in 141 characters?

I then thought, well if this is the next big thing, I better get on it and opened an account and started to send tweets, probably most of which, were totally useless!

But I soon realised the one thing that the big cheese of Social Media, Facebook, really focused on was friends.

So what happens when we make friends?

We build relationships and friendships and from this comes trust! The fundamental reason for your business carrying out the activity of marketing is to endeavor to build relationships with as many highly targeted prospects as possible so your prospects learn to trust you.

If there is a strong trust there is a significantly higher chance that your prospects will turn into paying customers!

When we talk to friends, we share information, we chat, we advise, we gossip and we build relationships.

When you start doing this, you can really build trust very quickly.

This is how Social Media can have an incredible impact on your business and on how you build relationships with your clients, quicker and better than ever before.

You can get to know and understand what your prospects and clients want and need and you can interact with them.

If you are writing articles, blogging and making informative and useful videos, people from all over the world can follow what you are doing.

You.... A Movie Star?!

Video is probably the most important task you should start thinking about more as it is the quickest way to get your message across.

These days, you don't need to spend a small fortune creating videos. It's more and more acceptable to have more of an amateur look to video and in my experience, if it is a "corporate" looking video with cheesy music and graphics, it actually turns people off!

You can buy a video camera for only £250 and start making short videos that are great for online marketing on your own website and you can also distribute them across dozens of videos sites.

You don't actually have to be a movie star to do it. I had a great tip from Tom Breeze, founder of TomBreeze.tv which was to write about a dozen of the top questions that your clients have asked you about your products and services.

Then have a colleague "interview" you and ask you those questions, to which you can already pre-plan your answers.

Its quick, easy and a great way for clients to really understand what you are doing and how your business can help them.

Social Media is changing how we do business. It is changing it in your town or city, in your marketplace and it is changing it NOW!

The potential gains for those who embrace Social Media are enormous, if it is done properly, consistently and relentlessly.

If I ask you to do one thing in this book it is not to miss the window of opportunity that is there right now to maximise on being an early adopter of Social Media in your business.

If you don't know what or how to do it, find a Social Media Manager who does.

At PrintRepublic, we have launched a Social Media Management division called TheSocialMediaRepublic.co.uk to handle this for clients for the following reason.

Most people either do not know what to do, or have no time to carry out a systematic Social Media campaign.

It is the fastest growing sector in my business.

We all thought the way the internet developed was fast. How all of a sudden it seemed to explode and we all wanted a piece of the action even though there are still many businesses those who are still poor at the implementation of an online strategy.

Well Social Media will be even quicker!

There will almost certainly be hundreds or possibly thousands of your potential clients who live and work not that far from where you are based who are on Facebook and Twitter today.

So why not start a conversation with them? It would surely be a little rude not to!

Now it depends on what market you are in, but I would be bold enough to speculate that if you own a small business, if you choose to embrace a Social Media strategy it will give you an unfair competitive advantage over the competition. We all love that don't we!

In so many markets, there is huge opportunity to dominate as the main sites are still comparatively young.

Social Media is an extremely efficient way of making more friends, building relationships and ultimately creating more customers!

If you look at it in this way, I am sure you will already be excited about implementing a Social Media Strategy now!

Twitter is everywhere now and is mentioned all over the place. From sportsmen who make rash statements on Twitter and get in trouble, to businesses and celebrities all over the world using it to make announcements and create awareness to what they are doing. Facebook has over 500 million users and growing every minute of every day. Just try and comprehend that number!

Blogging used to be an activity carried out by internet marketing specialists but now it seems everyone is doing it and the experts tell you it's essential to the future of your business. Everyone in business you ought to be on LinkedIn or you're just not happening!

Now this leads me back to what you do with friends.

We talk. We communicate and we tell each other what we have been doing or we are planning to do. It is a conversation.

So imagine if you just send a letter or an email, or post a brochure to a client. It's pretty much a one way conversation unless you hope a client responds in some way, but generally speaking it's a slow process. I still recommend you do it, but it's only part of what can be done.

With Social Media, you can make a statement and put out some information that everyone who you already have a relationship with can comment on instantly!

The beauty of this, it can become viral and they can tell everybody they know about what you are doing too!

In fact, people want this facility and they expect it. If you are not doing it, you're losing out!

This is the age of Social Media!

What is happening before our eyes is Social Media is changing the world. The fantastic opportunity is that the Small Business Owner can now compete with the big brands and corporate companies if Small Business Owners have the foresight to get involved – properly – right now.

The same thing is happening in Social Media as in all other new opportunities and new technologies that appear. There is a chance to make huge headway over your competition in your marketplace if you are quick off the blocks and you make it happen immediately.

If you don't embrace this opportunity you are missing a trick!

We all thought the internet was massive and it is, but what is happening now is that change is coming quicker than ever before so you have no time to waste!

The first thing you have to do is make the decision to do something about it.

If you are the type of person who is pretty savvy around Social Media outside of business, then it is pretty easy to focus on building an online reputation for your business too.

If you are not, then make sure you get help.

As I have said above, time is of the essence so there is a range of businesses out there who now specialise in helping businesses implement a Social Media strategy.

You just have to find one and hire them!

As I have mentioned, my business provides this service so if you are a UK business, just get in touch and I am sure we can help you.

But there are some other great people around too. As with everything I talk about in this book, there is always one common denominator which is to take action!

One thing that is important with a Social Media strategy is consistency, both in the message, style but also continuous delivery.

One blog post every quarter and a tweet every month is really not going to help! OK, it's a start, but you need to be doing building your online reputation and making new friends and contacts all the time!

If you really cannot do it all on your own because of time, knowledge or inclination, or simply you just don't know what to do... get someone to do it for you.

What will really invigorate and encourage you if you are doing this, is results can be seen very quickly.

Please don't misunderstand me. Social Media is not a sales platform for you to just try and flog your wares. It's the same as going to a party and meeting people. If you straightaway launch into a sales pitch to people you meet in a "social" environment, then you will turn people off very quickly.

The way I look at it is it's really just using common sense and social graces and manners! If you are natural, interesting, and not too pushy and you engage in 2-way conversation, then you will get to know more and more people and they will get to know you!

Social Media can be really fun and inspiring. I have connected with some amazing people through my social media pages. From celebrities to new employees, customers, and old faces I hadn't seen for many years.

CHAPTER THIRTEEN:

Raise the Bar

No I'm not talking about that classic Del Boy moment in British TV sitcom Only Fools and Horses when Del is attempting to look sophisticated and smooth, not realising a bar man has lifted the bar hatch, thus creating a hilarious moment of TV gold!

No I'm talking about setting goals in your business that are higher than you've ever done before.

Why settle for mediocrity when you can aim for greatness?

Now please don't misunderstand me here. I am not suggesting every business owner will be able to or want to be the next Richard Branson or one of the Dragons. Some people are really interested in developing a business that gives them a lifestyle not necessarily related to huge financial return.

But ultimately why are most people in business? It's pretty obvious, but it's to make money.

Having lots of money does not necessarily make you happy, but in my view, money does one vital thing over everything else and it is one of the primary reasons why I have always wanted my own business.

Money buys you choice.

Simple!

Having enough money to do whatever you want to do in your life puts you in the position that millions of people will envy.

For some it will be buying flash sports cars and taking luxurious holidays and for others it may just be the knowledge they have financial security to focus more time on their hobbies.

The important thing is to determine what you are trying to achieve and actually visualise how you deem success to be.

What does success look like in your head?

A good friend of mine is a good golfer and I am a particularly sporadic golfer! So whilst playing golf with him one day whilst we were in Spain on holiday, he saw my frustration at topping the ball and it rolling 50 yards behind a bush!

So he gave me a simple suggestion. Instead of just walking up to the ball, trying to smash the hell out of it and hoping for the best, stop, take time and think.

Actually visualise the shot in your head before you take it. Imagine the shot as you are addressing the ball, as you swing and then hit it perfectly and it lands directly where you are aiming.

So I tried it on my next shot and I know it sounds corny, but to my amazement I genuinely hit a lovely shot straight onto the green!

Now to you non golfers, I will not pretend life is perfect by explaining my putting in layman's terms... I cocked it up and 3 putted!

I always like to be realistic and I am more than aware that life has its ups and downs but what works for me is that visualisation in my head of the perfect golf shot that I know if I work hard enough, I will be able to achieve!

I guess one of my biggest strengths (and weaknesses too according to my wife!) is that I'm as stubborn as a mule!

I never give up!

I think in business this is a massive help and I don't give up if I believe I'm right.

One of my favourite (if most simple) quotes from Winston Churchill....

Never, ever, ever give up!

I don't think it is a great idea to flog a dead horse and sometimes it is actually crucial to know when you're beaten and to move on, but so many people give up at the first hurdle.

If you believe in what you do, you have done your research to know there is a gap in your market and you work out how you can tap into it, then drive on relentlessly and aim high!

The same goes for other parts of your life and especially your business.

If you just hope to get mediocre growth or hit easily achievable targets, guess what, that's all you will achieve!

Is that exciting and will you be over the moon if that's what you have aimed for?

Well if it's me, it wouldn't exactly get me whooping and hollering!

In my business and the goals I have in my life, I have possibly ridiculously high expectations. But I have eternal belief that if I aim that high, I will get there and if I only get somewhere near then I am going to have a hell of a lot of fun!

For me, isn't that what it's all about? A good friend of mine Wendy Shand who runs a fantastic travel business put it very succinctly when we met for one of our Mastermind Groups recently. Wendy said she approaches business like it is just a game. If you think of it as maybe a game of chess and every move you make has an impact on your position and the progress you make, it makes it feel a lot easier to be strategic in a much more informal and friendly way.

I am not really one to really talk in the corporate speak that you hear some people with occasionally highly inflated opinions of themselves talk in. I like to keep things simple and make sure I have my BS detector turned onto full!

I like to be a straight talker and approach business in this way and I have set my own goals with a simple, staged approach. I know what I want to earn each year and what my exit strategy is for each part of the business.

I have put some simple targets together and I have also visualised how I picture success.

I know the car I want to drive, the house I want to live in, the holidays I want to take, the amount of time I spend with my family.

I have an image of how my working week is, the type of team I have working in my business, the type of clients we have and the work we produce.

How have I done this?

There is one major step that Jonathan Jay, one of the leading Marketing Experts in the UK encouraged me to do, which was to take myself out of my business so I can work on it, not engrossed in day to day running.

This gives you a much clearer picture of what you are trying to achieve.

I have a great team of people and I have total faith in what they can deliver to our clients and that is a mistake I feel so many business owners fail to achieve. There is no worse a feeling than not having that trust in the people who work for you and if you are one of those control freaks who never lets their key people make a decision without you rubber stamping it, then you need to change and quickly otherwise you will turn yourself inside out!

Of course there are always key important decisions that as a business owner, you must make, but if you have a good team of people, empower them to make decisions in the knowledge that not all of them will be correct!

Has every decision you have ever made been right?

I seriously doubt it! If you are like me you will have made tonnes of wrong decisions but as long as you learn every time you do, you develop and get a little better each time.

As long as you make it clear to your team what decisions need referring to you and what decisions they can make for themselves, you then out trust in them and if they make a wrong decision, don't belittle them so they then live in fear of making another!

So set your own bar high, aim for the stars and you may well get to the moon!

What do I do now?

Well the first thing you need to do is to decide to **TAKE ACTION**! I am sure if you have read this book it has got you really thinking about how you can implement some or all of these ideas into your business and how your website can help you grow your sales and most importantly your PROFITS!

There are some things you need to consider and to decide what you need to do:-

1. Does my company logo and identity reflect the tone of the business I am in and does it sit well with the audience I am targeting?
2. Are my corporate identity and my marketing messages consistent throughout every touchpoint of my business, from my stationery, marketing literate and website, to maybe the packaging of my products, vehicle livery or anything that comes into contact with my customers and prospects?
3. Does my website tick all of the boxes discussed in this report?
4. Have I decided on my Social Media Strategy?
5. Have I set out my short, mid and long term goals?

OK, so if you decide you need to make some changes, what are the options for you?

1. Make the changes yourself

If you are technical and have the appropriate skills, you need to set aside the time to get started as a matter of urgency. You need to ensure you have continuity throughout all the items mentioned above and in this report. You can save yourself a bundle of money if you can do this which is great, but remember it can be very time consuming and you could be in danger of taking your eye of the ball of running your day to day business.

2. Do it yourself but get a little extra help

Maybe you've already got a good corporate identity but you need some new marketing literate – don't forget PrintRepublic! Perhaps your website is doing an ok job but you could do with a few tweaks so get onto your web developer and give precise instructions about what you want doing. Work with a couple of key suppliers to tweak what you have already got and you could get be underway very quickly. Set yourself a checklist of key criteria and work through it systematically.

3. Let PrintRepublic do all the hard work for you!

Yep I know that was a bit blatant though if you don't ask you don't get!! There are plenty of designers, web developers, copywriters and printers out there so take your pick but I hope you can see from this report, I know what I'm doing and I do stress the most important part is integrating all of your materials both on and offline and at PrintRepublic we specialise in providing the whole service to Small to Medium Sized Businesses.

If you already have some items ready and you are happy, for example your logo and corporate identity, but you need some new marketing literature produced and a new website built with an emarketing system integrated into it, then we'd be delighted to help.

The most important thing is to ACTUALLY TAKE ACTION AND DO IT...

TODAY!

Write down your Action List and go through how you want to proceed. Feel free to email it over for me to take a look – no obligation at all, I'd be happy to help and offer any advice I can.

Your Action Point List needs to include the following items:-

1. Your logo and identity
2. Your business cards
3. Company stationery
4. Promotional literature
5. Web Design
6. Free Report / Incentive
7. Irresistible Offers
8. E-marketing system and strategy
9. Guarantees
10. Headlines and call to Action
11. Email and Direct Mail Campaigns
12. Social Media Strategy
13. Raising my profile
14. Creating Video

I'd be delighted to give you some pointers if I can or do the whole project for you or at worst offer you some Free Business Cards!

Don't put off making a massive impact on your business today! Just take the first steps and make the decision todo it!

Good Luck

Stefan